COPYCAT

DRAWING BOOK
by
Sally Kilroy

10699

The Dial Press · New York

Published by The Dial Press
1 Dag Hammarskjold Plaza, New York, New York 10017

First published in Great Britain by Penguin Books Ltd.
Copyright © 1981 by Sally Kilroy. All rights reserved.
Printed in Great Britain. First U.S.A. printing.
ISBN 0-8037-1115-8   ISBN 0-8037-1116-6 lib. bdg.

THE SUN

Draw a yellow ball
with a happy face.

Add some lines around it
to show how bright it is.

AN UMBRELLA

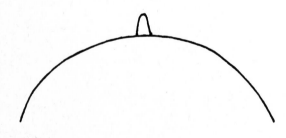 

Draw a big curve with a knob
in the middle.

Then draw three little curves
across the bottom.

CLOUDS AND RAIN

Join lots of curves together to make a white cloud –

or color the cloud gray and draw rain falling from it.

Draw two lines from the points to the knob.

Add a handle and color your umbrella.

A BIRD

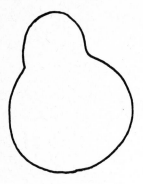  

| Draw a head and a body. | Add tail feathers and wings, | then eyes, a beak and feet. |

A GOLDFISH

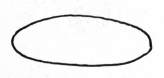 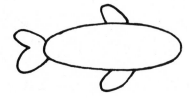 

Draw this shape. Add fins and a tail, then an eye and some scales. Color your fish.

When birds fly, they flap their wings and tuck up their feet.

When birds are far away in the sky, they look like this.

Then put it in a bowl.

Fill the bowl with water and draw some bubbles.

A CAT

Draw a head
with pointed ears.

Add eyes
and a nose,

now a mouth
and whiskers,

A MOUSE

Draw the body.

Add ears,

then eyes, a nose, and
some whiskers.

then a body.   Now draw legs and a tail,   and color your cat.

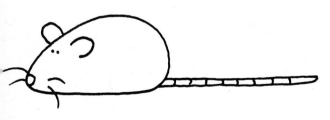

Now add a long tail

and some feet,
and then color your mouse.

AN ELEPHANT

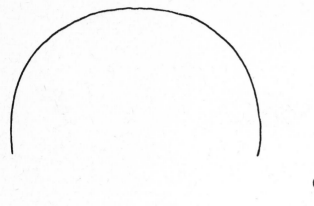 

Draw a big hump.

Add eyes, tusks, and a trunk,

A SNAKE

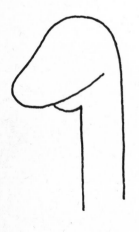  

Draw a head with a mouth and neck.

Add eyes and a forked tongue.

then big floppy ears
and a little tail.

Then draw the legs
and middle.
Now color your elephant.

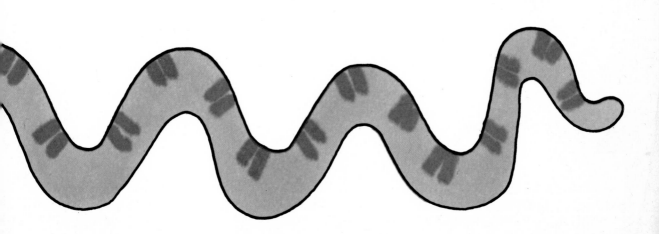

Draw a very long, wiggly body
and color it.

FACES

Draw this shape.

Add eyes, a nose,
a mouth,

and pink cheeks.

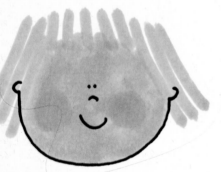

Draw some with
straight hair,

some with
curly hair,

and some with not much
hair at all.

Draw some faces with glasses.

Make faces happy,

Draw lots of faces and give them different hair.

Try a mustache

and a beard.

or sad,

or angry,

or even asleep.

MAKE FACES INTO PEOPLE

Give them necks,
then tops

and bottoms.

TRY DIFFERENT CLOTHES AND SHOES

Dungarees
to play in.

Draw T-shirts, shorts, and
sandals for the summer.

Now draw hands,

socks, and shoes.

Hats, slickers,
and boots
for the rain.

Woolly hats, scarves,
and mittens for
the winter.

A HOUSE

 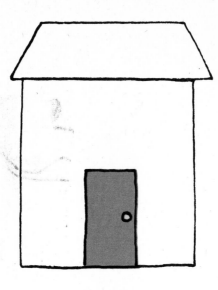 

Draw a box.

Add a roof
and a door,

then some windows.

A STREET

Try drawing lots of houses to make a street.

Now put shingles on the roof
and a chimney on top.

Add a path and some grass
and finish coloring your house.

Give them different roofs, doors, and windows.

A CLOCK

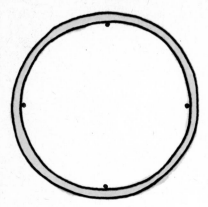 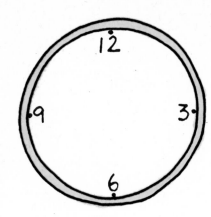 

Draw a yellow circle and make four dots at the top, bottom, and sides.

Put these numbers next to the dots.

Write the rest of the numbers. Add a big hand and a little hand.

A TELEPHONE

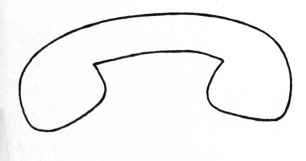 

Draw the receiver.

Then draw the base.

Now add a bell to make it
an alarm clock – or put it
in a long case to make a
grandfather clock.

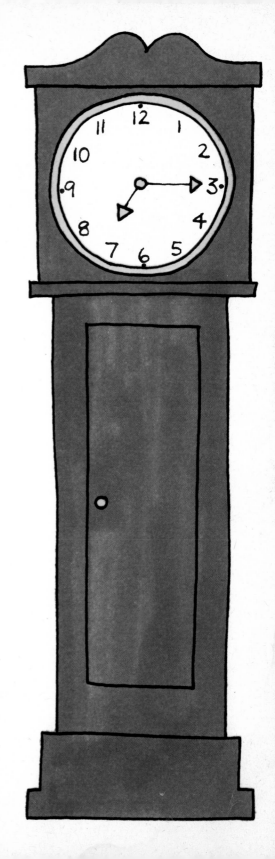

Now add the cord and the dial.
Put in the numbers.

CUPCAKES

Draw this shape.

Pour some frosting on top and add a cherry.

Now draw two more cupcakes and put all three of them on a plate.

A TEAPOT

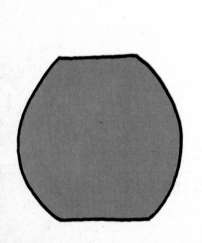 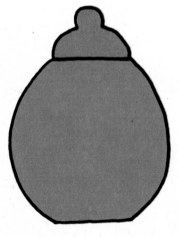 

Draw a circle with a flat top and bottom.

Add a lid,

then a spout and a handle.

A SODA

 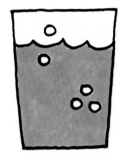  

Draw a glass.

Fill it with orange soda, add some bubbles

and then a striped straw.

A BIRTHDAY CAKE

Draw some candles on a big frosted cake and put it on a plate.

Then decorate the cake.

A HEN

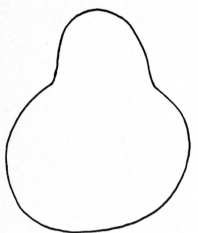

Draw a head and a body.

Add eyes, a beak,

and feathers.

A BOILED EGG

Draw an eggcup.

Put in an egg

and add a spoon.

Now sit the hen on a nest.

When she leaves the nest,
there might be some eggs.

Put them on a plate

and draw some toast.

AN APPLE

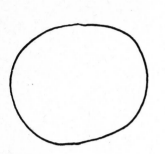  

Draw a circle.   Add a stalk   and a leaf,
                                             then color the apple.

A TREE

Join lots of curves together   Add a trunk and color the tree.
to make the top of a tree.

AN APPLE TREE

Draw the tree, then add some
apples before you color it.
Put some grass at the bottom.

A GATE

  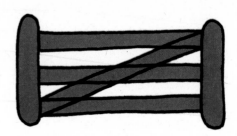

Draw two posts
this far apart.

Then add four bars like
this.

A FLOWER

Draw a small
yellow circle.

Put some petals
around it.

Then add a stem
and some leaves.

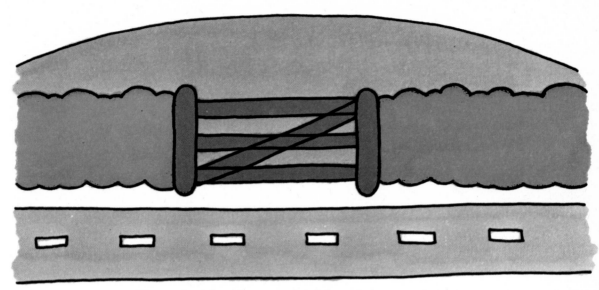

Draw bushes on each side of the gate.
Then draw a hill behind and a road in front.

You can put lots of flowers
together to make a plant

or arrange them in a vase.

A CASTLE

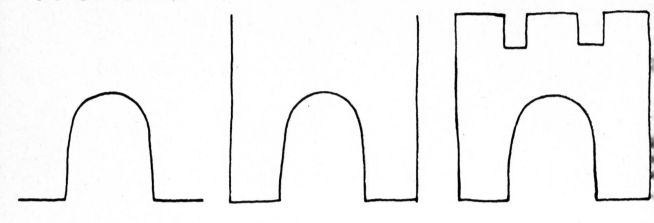

Draw this shape.

Then put up the walls

and draw the battlements along the top.

A WINDMILL

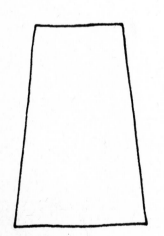

Draw this shape.

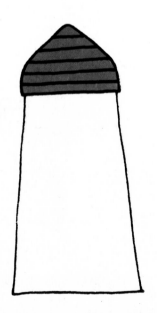

Add a curved roof,

then some windows and a door.

Now add a gate and slit windows.

Put the castle on a hilltop and add a flag.

Now draw a big X.

Add the sails and draw some grass around the windmill.

A CAR

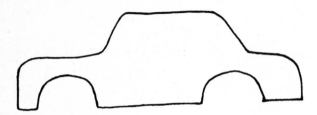 

Draw the body with
curves for the wheels.

Add windows
and a door,

A CRANE

Draw a cab
with a window
and a door.

Draw the tracks
and put the wheels
inside them.

Then add an arm with a chain
and a hook.
Put a driver in the cab.

then the wheels,
bumpers, and lights.

Put in a driver and color it all.

A TRUCK

Draw a cab with a window
and a big box behind.
Then add some wheels.

Add bumpers and lights,
then a driver and a
bright sign on the side.

AN AIRPLANE

Draw this shape.

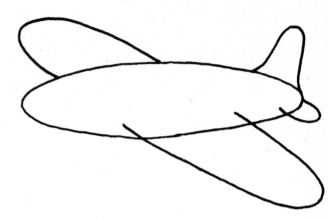

Add wings and a tail.

A SAILBOAT

Draw the boat with a mast and a flag.

Then draw one small sail and one big sail.

Then draw the jets
and windows.

Put some faces in the windows and
color everything.

Draw a sailor in the boat and
put it on the sea.

Add another boat and some birds
in the sky.

Try putting lots of things
from the book together
to make a big picture
like this.